The Bridal Checklists
BridalHandBook1

Copyright: Published in the United States by Rita L. Spears
Published September 2017

ISBN-13:978-1977593672

ISBN-10:1977593674

The Bridal Checklist

- ☐ Wedding Dress
- ☐ Veil & Hairpieces
- ☐ Shoes
- ☐ Necklace
- ☐ Earrings
- ☐ Other Jewelry
- ☐ Purse or Clutch
- ☐ Perfume
- ☐ Garter
- ☐ Wedding Rings

- ☐ Bouquets
- ☐ Invitations
- ☐ Ring Bearer Pillow
- ☐ Programs
- ☐ Gifts (From Groom)
- ☐ Other Keepsakes

The Bridal Checklist

- ☐ Wedding Dress
- ☐ Veil & Hairpieces
- ☐ Shoes
- ☐ Necklace
- ☐ Earrings
- ☐ Other Jewelry
- ☐ Purse or Clutch
- ☐ Perfume
- ☐ Garter
- ☐ Wedding Rings
- ☐ Bouquets
- ☐ Invitations
- ☐ Ring Bearer Pillow
- ☐ Programs
- ☐ Gifts (From Groom)
- ☐ Other Keepsakes

The Bridal Checklist

☐ Wedding Dress

☐ Veil & Hairpieces

☐ Shoes

☐ Necklace

☐ Earrings

☐ Other Jewelry

☐ Purse or Clutch

☐ Perfume

☐ Garter

☐ Wedding Rings

☐ Bouquets

☐ Invitations

☐ Ring Bearer Pillow

☐ Programs

☐ Gifts (From Groom)

☐ Other Keepsakes

The Bridal Checklist

- ☐ Wedding Dress
- ☐ Veil & Hairpieces
- ☐ Shoes
- ☐ Necklace
- ☐ Earrings
- ☐ Other Jewelry
- ☐ Purse or Clutch
- ☐ Perfume
- ☐ Garter
- ☐ Wedding Rings

- ☐ Bouquets
- ☐ Invitations
- ☐ Ring Bearer Pillow
- ☐ Programs
- ☐ Gifts (From Groom)
- ☐ Other Keepsakes

The Bridal Checklist

- ☐ Wedding Dress
- ☐ Veil & Hairpieces
- ☐ Shoes
- ☐ Necklace
- ☐ Earrings
- ☐ Other Jewelry
- ☐ Purse or Clutch
- ☐ Perfume
- ☐ Garter
- ☐ Wedding Rings

- ☐ Bouquets
- ☐ Invitations
- ☐ Ring Bearer Pillow
- ☐ Programs
- ☐ Gifts (From Groom)
- ☐ Other Keepsakes

The Bridal Checklist

- ☐ Wedding Dress
- ☐ Veil & Hairpieces
- ☐ Shoes
- ☐ Necklace
- ☐ Earrings
- ☐ Other Jewelry
- ☐ Purse or Clutch
- ☐ Perfume
- ☐ Garter
- ☐ Wedding Rings

- ☐ Bouquets
- ☐ Invitations
- ☐ Ring Bearer Pillow
- ☐ Programs
- ☐ Gifts (From Groom)
- ☐ Other Keepsakes

The Bridal Checklist

- ☐ Wedding Dress
- ☐ Veil & Hairpieces
- ☐ Shoes
- ☐ Necklace
- ☐ Earrings
- ☐ Other Jewelry
- ☐ Purse or Clutch
- ☐ Perfume
- ☐ Garter
- ☐ Wedding Rings

- ☐ Bouquets
- ☐ Invitations
- ☐ Ring Bearer Pillow
- ☐ Programs
- ☐ Gifts (From Groom)
- ☐ Other Keepsakes

The Bridal Checklist

- ☐ Wedding Dress
- ☐ Veil & Hairpieces
- ☐ Shoes
- ☐ Necklace
- ☐ Earrings
- ☐ Other Jewelry
- ☐ Purse or Clutch
- ☐ Perfume
- ☐ Garter
- ☐ Wedding Rings

- ☐ Bouquets
- ☐ Invitations
- ☐ Ring Bearer Pillow
- ☐ Programs
- ☐ Gifts (From Groom)
- ☐ Other Keepsakes

The Bridal Checklist

- ☐ Wedding Dress
- ☐ Veil & Hairpieces
- ☐ Shoes
- ☐ Necklace
- ☐ Earrings
- ☐ Other Jewelry
- ☐ Purse or Clutch
- ☐ Perfume
- ☐ Garter
- ☐ Wedding Rings

- ☐ Bouquets
- ☐ Invitations
- ☐ Ring Bearer Pillow
- ☐ Programs
- ☐ Gifts (From Groom)
- ☐ Other Keepsakes

The Bridal Checklist

- ☐ Wedding Dress
- ☐ Veil & Hairpieces
- ☐ Shoes
- ☐ Necklace
- ☐ Earrings
- ☐ Other Jewelry
- ☐ Purse or Clutch
- ☐ Perfume
- ☐ Garter
- ☐ Wedding Rings

- ☐ Bouquets
- ☐ Invitations
- ☐ Ring Bearer Pillow
- ☐ Programs
- ☐ Gifts (From Groom)
- ☐ Other Keepsakes

The Bridal Checklist

- ☐ Wedding Dress
- ☐ Veil & Hairpieces
- ☐ Shoes
- ☐ Necklace
- ☐ Earrings
- ☐ Other Jewelry
- ☐ Purse or Clutch
- ☐ Perfume
- ☐ Garter
- ☐ Wedding Rings
- ☐ Bouquets
- ☐ Invitations
- ☐ Ring Bearer Pillow
- ☐ Programs
- ☐ Gifts (From Groom)
- ☐ Other Keepsakes

The Bridal Checklist

- ☐ Wedding Dress
- ☐ Veil & Hairpieces
- ☐ Shoes
- ☐ Necklace
- ☐ Earrings
- ☐ Other Jewelry
- ☐ Purse or Clutch
- ☐ Perfume
- ☐ Garter
- ☐ Wedding Rings

- ☐ Bouquets
- ☐ Invitations
- ☐ Ring Bearer Pillow
- ☐ Programs
- ☐ Gifts (From Groom)
- ☐ Other Keepsakes

The Bridal Checklist

- ☐ Wedding Dress
- ☐ Veil & Hairpieces
- ☐ Shoes
- ☐ Necklace
- ☐ Earrings
- ☐ Other Jewelry
- ☐ Purse or Clutch
- ☐ Perfume
- ☐ Garter
- ☐ Wedding Rings

- ☐ Bouquets
- ☐ Invitations
- ☐ Ring Bearer Pillow
- ☐ Programs
- ☐ Gifts (From Groom)
- ☐ Other Keepsakes

The Bridal Checklist

- ☐ Wedding Dress
- ☐ Veil & Hairpieces
- ☐ Shoes
- ☐ Necklace
- ☐ Earrings
- ☐ Other Jewelry
- ☐ Purse or Clutch
- ☐ Perfume
- ☐ Garter
- ☐ Wedding Rings

- ☐ Bouquets
- ☐ Invitations
- ☐ Ring Bearer Pillow
- ☐ Programs
- ☐ Gifts (From Groom)
- ☐ Other Keepsakes

The Bridal Checklist

- ☐ Wedding Dress
- ☐ Veil & Hairpieces
- ☐ Shoes
- ☐ Necklace
- ☐ Earrings
- ☐ Other Jewelry
- ☐ Purse or Clutch
- ☐ Perfume
- ☐ Garter
- ☐ Wedding Rings

- ☐ Bouquets
- ☐ Invitations
- ☐ Ring Bearer Pillow
- ☐ Programs
- ☐ Gifts (From Groom)
- ☐ Other Keepsakes

The Bridal Checklist

- ☐ Wedding Dress
- ☐ Veil & Hairpieces
- ☐ Shoes
- ☐ Necklace
- ☐ Earrings
- ☐ Other Jewelry
- ☐ Purse or Clutch
- ☐ Perfume
- ☐ Garter
- ☐ Wedding Rings

- ☐ Bouquets
- ☐ Invitations
- ☐ Ring Bearer Pillow
- ☐ Programs
- ☐ Gifts (From Groom)
- ☐ Other Keepsakes

The Bridal Checklist

- ☐ Wedding Dress
- ☐ Veil & Hairpieces
- ☐ Shoes
- ☐ Necklace
- ☐ Earrings
- ☐ Other Jewelry
- ☐ Purse or Clutch
- ☐ Perfume
- ☐ Garter
- ☐ Wedding Rings

- ☐ Bouquets
- ☐ Invitations
- ☐ Ring Bearer Pillow
- ☐ Programs
- ☐ Gifts (From Groom)
- ☐ Other Keepsakes

The Bridal Checklist

- ☐ Wedding Dress
- ☐ Veil & Hairpieces
- ☐ Shoes
- ☐ Necklace
- ☐ Earrings
- ☐ Other Jewelry
- ☐ Purse or Clutch
- ☐ Perfume
- ☐ Garter
- ☐ Wedding Rings

- ☐ Bouquets
- ☐ Invitations
- ☐ Ring Bearer Pillow
- ☐ Programs
- ☐ Gifts (From Groom)
- ☐ Other Keepsakes

The Bridal Checklist

- ☐ Wedding Dress
- ☐ Veil & Hairpieces
- ☐ Shoes
- ☐ Necklace
- ☐ Earrings
- ☐ Other Jewelry
- ☐ Purse or Clutch
- ☐ Perfume
- ☐ Garter
- ☐ Wedding Rings
- ☐ Bouquets
- ☐ Invitations
- ☐ Ring Bearer Pillow
- ☐ Programs
- ☐ Gifts (From Groom)
- ☐ Other Keepsakes

The Bridal Checklist

- ☐ Wedding Dress
- ☐ Veil & Hairpieces
- ☐ Shoes
- ☐ Necklace
- ☐ Earrings
- ☐ Other Jewelry
- ☐ Purse or Clutch
- ☐ Perfume
- ☐ Garter
- ☐ Wedding Rings

- ☐ Bouquets
- ☐ Invitations
- ☐ Ring Bearer Pillow
- ☐ Programs
- ☐ Gifts (From Groom)
- ☐ Other Keepsakes

The Bridal Checklist

- [ ] Wedding Dress
- [ ] Veil & Hairpieces
- [ ] Shoes
- [ ] Necklace
- [ ] Earrings
- [ ] Other Jewelry
- [ ] Purse or Clutch
- [ ] Perfume
- [ ] Garter
- [ ] Wedding Rings
- [ ] Bouquets
- [ ] Invitations
- [ ] Ring Bearer Pillow
- [ ] Programs
- [ ] Gifts (From Groom)
- [ ] Other Keepsakes

The Bridal Checklist

- [ ] Wedding Dress
- [ ] Veil & Hairpieces
- [ ] Shoes
- [ ] Necklace
- [ ] Earrings
- [ ] Other Jewelry
- [ ] Purse or Clutch
- [ ] Perfume
- [ ] Garter
- [ ] Wedding Rings

- [ ] Bouquets
- [ ] Invitations
- [ ] Ring Bearer Pillow
- [ ] Programs
- [ ] Gifts (From Groom)
- [ ] Other Keepsakes

The Bridal Checklist

- ☐ Wedding Dress
- ☐ Veil & Hairpieces
- ☐ Shoes
- ☐ Necklace
- ☐ Earrings
- ☐ Other Jewelry
- ☐ Purse or Clutch
- ☐ Perfume
- ☐ Garter
- ☐ Wedding Rings
- ☐ Bouquets
- ☐ Invitations
- ☐ Ring Bearer Pillow
- ☐ Programs
- ☐ Gifts (From Groom)
- ☐ Other Keepsakes

The Bridal Checklist

- ☐ Wedding Dress
- ☐ Veil & Hairpieces
- ☐ Shoes
- ☐ Necklace
- ☐ Earrings
- ☐ Other Jewelry
- ☐ Purse or Clutch
- ☐ Perfume
- ☐ Garter
- ☐ Wedding Rings

- ☐ Bouquets
- ☐ Invitations
- ☐ Ring Bearer Pillow
- ☐ Programs
- ☐ Gifts (From Groom)
- ☐ Other Keepsakes

The Bridal Checklist

- ☐ Wedding Dress
- ☐ Veil & Hairpieces
- ☐ Shoes
- ☐ Necklace
- ☐ Earrings
- ☐ Other Jewelry
- ☐ Purse or Clutch
- ☐ Perfume
- ☐ Garter
- ☐ Wedding Rings

- ☐ Bouquets
- ☐ Invitations
- ☐ Ring Bearer Pillow
- ☐ Programs
- ☐ Gifts (From Groom)
- ☐ Other Keepsakes

The Bridal Checklist

<table>
<tr><td>☐ Wedding Dress</td><td>☐ Bouquets</td></tr>
<tr><td>☐ Veil & Hairpieces</td><td>☐ Invitations</td></tr>
<tr><td>☐ Shoes</td><td>☐ Ring Bearer Pillow</td></tr>
<tr><td>☐ Necklace</td><td>☐ Programs</td></tr>
<tr><td>☐ Earrings</td><td>☐ Gifts (From Groom)</td></tr>
<tr><td>☐ Other Jewelry</td><td>☐ Other Keepsakes</td></tr>
<tr><td>☐ Purse or Clutch</td><td></td></tr>
<tr><td>☐ Perfume</td><td></td></tr>
<tr><td>☐ Garter</td><td></td></tr>
<tr><td>☐ Wedding Rings</td><td></td></tr>
</table>

The Bridal Checklist

- [ ] Wedding Dress
- [ ] Veil & Hairpieces
- [ ] Shoes
- [ ] Necklace
- [ ] Earrings
- [ ] Other Jewelry
- [ ] Purse or Clutch
- [ ] Perfume
- [ ] Garter
- [ ] Wedding Rings

- [ ] Bouquets
- [ ] Invitations
- [ ] Ring Bearer Pillow
- [ ] Programs
- [ ] Gifts (From Groom)
- [ ] Other Keepsakes

The Bridal Checklist

- ☐ Wedding Dress
- ☐ Veil & Hairpieces
- ☐ Shoes
- ☐ Necklace
- ☐ Earrings
- ☐ Other Jewelry
- ☐ Purse or Clutch
- ☐ Perfume
- ☐ Garter
- ☐ Wedding Rings

- ☐ Bouquets
- ☐ Invitations
- ☐ Ring Bearer Pillow
- ☐ Programs
- ☐ Gifts (From Groom)
- ☐ Other Keepsakes

The Bridal Checklist

<table>
<tr><td>☐ Wedding Dress</td><td>☐ Bouquets</td></tr>
<tr><td>☐ Veil & Hairpieces</td><td>☐ Invitations</td></tr>
<tr><td>☐ Shoes</td><td>☐ Ring Bearer Pillow</td></tr>
<tr><td>☐ Necklace</td><td>☐ Programs</td></tr>
<tr><td>☐ Earrings</td><td>☐ Gifts (From Groom)</td></tr>
<tr><td>☐ Other Jewelry</td><td>☐ Other Keepsakes</td></tr>
<tr><td>☐ Purse or Clutch</td><td></td></tr>
<tr><td>☐ Perfume</td><td></td></tr>
<tr><td>☐ Garter</td><td></td></tr>
<tr><td>☐ Wedding Rings</td><td></td></tr>
</table>

The Bridal Checklist

- ☐ Wedding Dress
- ☐ Veil & Hairpieces
- ☐ Shoes
- ☐ Necklace
- ☐ Earrings
- ☐ Other Jewelry
- ☐ Purse or Clutch
- ☐ Perfume
- ☐ Garter
- ☐ Wedding Rings

- ☐ Bouquets
- ☐ Invitations
- ☐ Ring Bearer Pillow
- ☐ Programs
- ☐ Gifts (From Groom)
- ☐ Other Keepsakes

The Bridal Checklist

- ☐ Wedding Dress
- ☐ Veil & Hairpieces
- ☐ Shoes
- ☐ Necklace
- ☐ Earrings
- ☐ Other Jewelry
- ☐ Purse or Clutch
- ☐ Perfume
- ☐ Garter
- ☐ Wedding Rings
- ☐ Bouquets
- ☐ Invitations
- ☐ Ring Bearer Pillow
- ☐ Programs
- ☐ Gifts (From Groom)
- ☐ Other Keepsakes

The Bridal Checklist

- ☐ Wedding Dress
- ☐ Veil & Hairpieces
- ☐ Shoes
- ☐ Necklace
- ☐ Earrings
- ☐ Other Jewelry
- ☐ Purse or Clutch
- ☐ Perfume
- ☐ Garter
- ☐ Wedding Rings

- ☐ Bouquets
- ☐ Invitations
- ☐ Ring Bearer Pillow
- ☐ Programs
- ☐ Gifts (From Groom)
- ☐ Other Keepsakes

The Bridal Checklist

☐ Wedding Dress	☐ Bouquets
☐ Veil & Hairpieces	☐ Invitations
☐ Shoes	☐ Ring Bearer Pillow
☐ Necklace	☐ Programs
☐ Earrings	☐ Gifts (From Groom)
☐ Other Jewelry	☐ Other Keepsakes
☐ Purse or Clutch	
☐ Perfume	
☐ Garter	
☐ Wedding Rings	

The Bridal Checklist

- [ ] Wedding Dress
- [ ] Veil & Hairpieces
- [ ] Shoes
- [ ] Necklace
- [ ] Earrings
- [ ] Other Jewelry
- [ ] Purse or Clutch
- [ ] Perfume
- [ ] Garter
- [ ] Wedding Rings

- [ ] Bouquets
- [ ] Invitations
- [ ] Ring Bearer Pillow
- [ ] Programs
- [ ] Gifts (From Groom)
- [ ] Other Keepsakes

The Bridal Checklist

- ☐ Wedding Dress
- ☐ Veil & Hairpieces
- ☐ Shoes
- ☐ Necklace
- ☐ Earrings
- ☐ Other Jewelry
- ☐ Purse or Clutch
- ☐ Perfume
- ☐ Garter
- ☐ Wedding Rings

- ☐ Bouquets
- ☐ Invitations
- ☐ Ring Bearer Pillow
- ☐ Programs
- ☐ Gifts (From Groom)
- ☐ Other Keepsakes

The Bridal Checklist

- ☐ Wedding Dress
- ☐ Veil & Hairpieces
- ☐ Shoes
- ☐ Necklace
- ☐ Earrings
- ☐ Other Jewelry
- ☐ Purse or Clutch
- ☐ Perfume
- ☐ Garter
- ☐ Wedding Rings

- ☐ Bouquets
- ☐ Invitations
- ☐ Ring Bearer Pillow
- ☐ Programs
- ☐ Gifts (From Groom)
- ☐ Other Keepsakes

The Bridal Checklist

- ☐ Wedding Dress
- ☐ Veil & Hairpieces
- ☐ Shoes
- ☐ Necklace
- ☐ Earrings
- ☐ Other Jewelry
- ☐ Purse or Clutch
- ☐ Perfume
- ☐ Garter
- ☐ Wedding Rings

- ☐ Bouquets
- ☐ Invitations
- ☐ Ring Bearer Pillow
- ☐ Programs
- ☐ Gifts (From Groom)
- ☐ Other Keepsakes

The Bridal Checklist

- ☐ Wedding Dress
- ☐ Veil & Hairpieces
- ☐ Shoes
- ☐ Necklace
- ☐ Earrings
- ☐ Other Jewelry
- ☐ Purse or Clutch
- ☐ Perfume
- ☐ Garter
- ☐ Wedding Rings

- ☐ Bouquets
- ☐ Invitations
- ☐ Ring Bearer Pillow
- ☐ Programs
- ☐ Gifts (From Groom)
- ☐ Other Keepsakes

The Bridal Checklist

- ☐ Wedding Dress
- ☐ Veil & Hairpieces
- ☐ Shoes
- ☐ Necklace
- ☐ Earrings
- ☐ Other Jewelry
- ☐ Purse or Clutch
- ☐ Perfume
- ☐ Garter
- ☐ Wedding Rings

- ☐ Bouquets
- ☐ Invitations
- ☐ Ring Bearer Pillow
- ☐ Programs
- ☐ Gifts (From Groom)
- ☐ Other Keepsakes

The Bridal Checklist

- ☐ Wedding Dress
- ☐ Veil & Hairpieces
- ☐ Shoes
- ☐ Necklace
- ☐ Earrings
- ☐ Other Jewelry
- ☐ Purse or Clutch
- ☐ Perfume
- ☐ Garter
- ☐ Wedding Rings

- ☐ Bouquets
- ☐ Invitations
- ☐ Ring Bearer Pillow
- ☐ Programs
- ☐ Gifts (From Groom)
- ☐ Other Keepsakes

The Bridal Checklist

- ☐ Wedding Dress
- ☐ Veil & Hairpieces
- ☐ Shoes
- ☐ Necklace
- ☐ Earrings
- ☐ Other Jewelry
- ☐ Purse or Clutch
- ☐ Perfume
- ☐ Garter
- ☐ Wedding Rings

- ☐ Bouquets
- ☐ Invitations
- ☐ Ring Bearer Pillow
- ☐ Programs
- ☐ Gifts (From Groom)
- ☐ Other Keepsakes

The Bridal Checklist

- ☐ Wedding Dress
- ☐ Veil & Hairpieces
- ☐ Shoes
- ☐ Necklace
- ☐ Earrings
- ☐ Other Jewelry
- ☐ Purse or Clutch
- ☐ Perfume
- ☐ Garter
- ☐ Wedding Rings

- ☐ Bouquets
- ☐ Invitations
- ☐ Ring Bearer Pillow
- ☐ Programs
- ☐ Gifts (From Groom)
- ☐ Other Keepsakes

The Bridal Checklist

- ☐ Wedding Dress
- ☐ Veil & Hairpieces
- ☐ Shoes
- ☐ Necklace
- ☐ Earrings
- ☐ Other Jewelry
- ☐ Purse or Clutch
- ☐ Perfume
- ☐ Garter
- ☐ Wedding Rings

- ☐ Bouquets
- ☐ Invitations
- ☐ Ring Bearer Pillow
- ☐ Programs
- ☐ Gifts (From Groom)
- ☐ Other Keepsakes

The Bridal Checklist

- ☐ Wedding Dress
- ☐ Veil & Hairpieces
- ☐ Shoes
- ☐ Necklace
- ☐ Earrings
- ☐ Other Jewelry
- ☐ Purse or Clutch
- ☐ Perfume
- ☐ Garter
- ☐ Wedding Rings
- ☐ Bouquets
- ☐ Invitations
- ☐ Ring Bearer Pillow
- ☐ Programs
- ☐ Gifts (From Groom)
- ☐ Other Keepsakes

The Bridal Checklist

- ☐ Wedding Dress
- ☐ Veil & Hairpieces
- ☐ Shoes
- ☐ Necklace
- ☐ Earrings
- ☐ Other Jewelry
- ☐ Purse or Clutch
- ☐ Perfume
- ☐ Garter
- ☐ Wedding Rings

- ☐ Bouquets
- ☐ Invitations
- ☐ Ring Bearer Pillow
- ☐ Programs
- ☐ Gifts (From Groom)
- ☐ Other Keepsakes

The Bridal Checklist

- ☐ Wedding Dress
- ☐ Veil & Hairpieces
- ☐ Shoes
- ☐ Necklace
- ☐ Earrings
- ☐ Other Jewelry
- ☐ Purse or Clutch
- ☐ Perfume
- ☐ Garter
- ☐ Wedding Rings

- ☐ Bouquets
- ☐ Invitations
- ☐ Ring Bearer Pillow
- ☐ Programs
- ☐ Gifts (From Groom)
- ☐ Other Keepsakes

The Bridal Checklist

- ☐ Wedding Dress
- ☐ Veil & Hairpieces
- ☐ Shoes
- ☐ Necklace
- ☐ Earrings
- ☐ Other Jewelry
- ☐ Purse or Clutch
- ☐ Perfume
- ☐ Garter
- ☐ Wedding Rings
- ☐ Bouquets
- ☐ Invitations
- ☐ Ring Bearer Pillow
- ☐ Programs
- ☐ Gifts (From Groom)
- ☐ Other Keepsakes

The Bridal Checklist

- ☐ Wedding Dress
- ☐ Veil & Hairpieces
- ☐ Shoes
- ☐ Necklace
- ☐ Earrings
- ☐ Other Jewelry
- ☐ Purse or Clutch
- ☐ Perfume
- ☐ Garter
- ☐ Wedding Rings

- ☐ Bouquets
- ☐ Invitations
- ☐ Ring Bearer Pillow
- ☐ Programs
- ☐ Gifts (From Groom)
- ☐ Other Keepsakes

The Bridal Checklist

- ☐ Wedding Dress
- ☐ Veil & Hairpieces
- ☐ Shoes
- ☐ Necklace
- ☐ Earrings
- ☐ Other Jewelry
- ☐ Purse or Clutch
- ☐ Perfume
- ☐ Garter
- ☐ Wedding Rings

- ☐ Bouquets
- ☐ Invitations
- ☐ Ring Bearer Pillow
- ☐ Programs
- ☐ Gifts (From Groom)
- ☐ Other Keepsakes

The Bridal Checklist

- ☐ Wedding Dress
- ☐ Veil & Hairpieces
- ☐ Shoes
- ☐ Necklace
- ☐ Earrings
- ☐ Other Jewelry
- ☐ Purse or Clutch
- ☐ Perfume
- ☐ Garter
- ☐ Wedding Rings

- ☐ Bouquets
- ☐ Invitations
- ☐ Ring Bearer Pillow
- ☐ Programs
- ☐ Gifts (From Groom)
- ☐ Other Keepsakes

The Bridal Checklist

- ☐ Wedding Dress
- ☐ Veil & Hairpieces
- ☐ Shoes
- ☐ Necklace
- ☐ Earrings
- ☐ Other Jewelry
- ☐ Purse or Clutch
- ☐ Perfume
- ☐ Garter
- ☐ Wedding Rings
- ☐ Bouquets
- ☐ Invitations
- ☐ Ring Bearer Pillow
- ☐ Programs
- ☐ Gifts (From Groom)
- ☐ Other Keepsakes

The Bridal Checklist

- ☐ Wedding Dress
- ☐ Veil & Hairpieces
- ☐ Shoes
- ☐ Necklace
- ☐ Earrings
- ☐ Other Jewelry
- ☐ Purse or Clutch
- ☐ Perfume
- ☐ Garter
- ☐ Wedding Rings

- ☐ Bouquets
- ☐ Invitations
- ☐ Ring Bearer Pillow
- ☐ Programs
- ☐ Gifts (From Groom)
- ☐ Other Keepsakes

The Bridal Checklist

- ☐ Wedding Dress
- ☐ Veil & Hairpieces
- ☐ Shoes
- ☐ Necklace
- ☐ Earrings
- ☐ Other Jewelry
- ☐ Purse or Clutch
- ☐ Perfume
- ☐ Garter
- ☐ Wedding Rings

- ☐ Bouquets
- ☐ Invitations
- ☐ Ring Bearer Pillow
- ☐ Programs
- ☐ Gifts (From Groom)
- ☐ Other Keepsakes

The Bridal Checklist

<table>
<tr><td>☐ Wedding Dress</td><td>☐ Bouquets</td></tr>
<tr><td>☐ Veil & Hairpieces</td><td>☐ Invitations</td></tr>
<tr><td>☐ Shoes</td><td>☐ Ring Bearer Pillow</td></tr>
<tr><td>☐ Necklace</td><td>☐ Programs</td></tr>
<tr><td>☐ Earrings</td><td>☐ Gifts (From Groom)</td></tr>
<tr><td>☐ Other Jewelry</td><td>☐ Other Keepsakes</td></tr>
<tr><td>☐ Purse or Clutch</td><td></td></tr>
<tr><td>☐ Perfume</td><td></td></tr>
<tr><td>☐ Garter</td><td></td></tr>
<tr><td>☐ Wedding Rings</td><td></td></tr>
</table>

The Bridal Checklist

- ☐ Wedding Dress
- ☐ Veil & Hairpieces
- ☐ Shoes
- ☐ Necklace
- ☐ Earrings
- ☐ Other Jewelry
- ☐ Purse or Clutch
- ☐ Perfume
- ☐ Garter
- ☐ Wedding Rings

- ☐ Bouquets
- ☐ Invitations
- ☐ Ring Bearer Pillow
- ☐ Programs
- ☐ Gifts (From Groom)
- ☐ Other Keepsakes

The Bridal Checklist

- ☐ Wedding Dress
- ☐ Veil & Hairpieces
- ☐ Shoes
- ☐ Necklace
- ☐ Earrings
- ☐ Other Jewelry
- ☐ Purse or Clutch
- ☐ Perfume
- ☐ Garter
- ☐ Wedding Rings

- ☐ Bouquets
- ☐ Invitations
- ☐ Ring Bearer Pillow
- ☐ Programs
- ☐ Gifts (From Groom)
- ☐ Other Keepsakes

The Bridal Checklist

- ☐ Wedding Dress
- ☐ Veil & Hairpieces
- ☐ Shoes
- ☐ Necklace
- ☐ Earrings
- ☐ Other Jewelry
- ☐ Purse or Clutch
- ☐ Perfume
- ☐ Garter
- ☐ Wedding Rings

- ☐ Bouquets
- ☐ Invitations
- ☐ Ring Bearer Pillow
- ☐ Programs
- ☐ Gifts (From Groom)
- ☐ Other Keepsakes

The Bridal Checklist

<table>
<tr><td>☐ Wedding Dress</td><td>☐ Bouquets</td></tr>
<tr><td>☐ Veil & Hairpieces</td><td>☐ Invitations</td></tr>
<tr><td>☐ Shoes</td><td>☐ Ring Bearer Pillow</td></tr>
<tr><td>☐ Necklace</td><td>☐ Programs</td></tr>
<tr><td>☐ Earrings</td><td>☐ Gifts (From Groom)</td></tr>
<tr><td>☐ Other Jewelry</td><td>☐ Other Keepsakes</td></tr>
<tr><td>☐ Purse or Clutch</td><td></td></tr>
<tr><td>☐ Perfume</td><td></td></tr>
<tr><td>☐ Garter</td><td></td></tr>
<tr><td>☐ Wedding Rings</td><td></td></tr>
</table>

The Bridal Checklist

- ☐ Wedding Dress
- ☐ Veil & Hairpieces
- ☐ Shoes
- ☐ Necklace
- ☐ Earrings
- ☐ Other Jewelry
- ☐ Purse or Clutch
- ☐ Perfume
- ☐ Garter
- ☐ Wedding Rings

- ☐ Bouquets
- ☐ Invitations
- ☐ Ring Bearer Pillow
- ☐ Programs
- ☐ Gifts (From Groom)
- ☐ Other Keepsakes

The Bridal Checklist

- ☐ Wedding Dress
- ☐ Veil & Hairpieces
- ☐ Shoes
- ☐ Necklace
- ☐ Earrings
- ☐ Other Jewelry
- ☐ Purse or Clutch
- ☐ Perfume
- ☐ Garter
- ☐ Wedding Rings

- ☐ Bouquets
- ☐ Invitations
- ☐ Ring Bearer Pillow
- ☐ Programs
- ☐ Gifts (From Groom)
- ☐ Other Keepsakes

The Bridal Checklist

- [ ] Wedding Dress
- [ ] Veil & Hairpieces
- [ ] Shoes
- [ ] Necklace
- [ ] Earrings
- [ ] Other Jewelry
- [ ] Purse or Clutch
- [ ] Perfume
- [ ] Garter
- [ ] Wedding Rings

- [ ] Bouquets
- [ ] Invitations
- [ ] Ring Bearer Pillow
- [ ] Programs
- [ ] Gifts (From Groom)
- [ ] Other Keepsakes

The Bridal Checklist

- ☐ Wedding Dress
- ☐ Veil & Hairpieces
- ☐ Shoes
- ☐ Necklace
- ☐ Earrings
- ☐ Other Jewelry
- ☐ Purse or Clutch
- ☐ Perfume
- ☐ Garter
- ☐ Wedding Rings

- ☐ Bouquets
- ☐ Invitations
- ☐ Ring Bearer Pillow
- ☐ Programs
- ☐ Gifts (From Groom)
- ☐ Other Keepsakes

The Bridal Checklist

- [ ] Wedding Dress
- [ ] Veil & Hairpieces
- [ ] Shoes
- [ ] Necklace
- [ ] Earrings
- [ ] Other Jewelry
- [ ] Purse or Clutch
- [ ] Perfume
- [ ] Garter
- [ ] Wedding Rings

- [ ] Bouquets
- [ ] Invitations
- [ ] Ring Bearer Pillow
- [ ] Programs
- [ ] Gifts (From Groom)
- [ ] Other Keepsakes

The Bridal Checklist

- [ ] Wedding Dress
- [ ] Veil & Hairpieces
- [ ] Shoes
- [ ] Necklace
- [ ] Earrings
- [ ] Other Jewelry
- [ ] Purse or Clutch
- [ ] Perfume
- [ ] Garter
- [ ] Wedding Rings

- [ ] Bouquets
- [ ] Invitations
- [ ] Ring Bearer Pillow
- [ ] Programs
- [ ] Gifts (From Groom)
- [ ] Other Keepsakes

The Bridal Checklist

- ☐ Wedding Dress
- ☐ Veil & Hairpieces
- ☐ Shoes
- ☐ Necklace
- ☐ Earrings
- ☐ Other Jewelry
- ☐ Purse or Clutch
- ☐ Perfume
- ☐ Garter
- ☐ Wedding Rings

- ☐ Bouquets
- ☐ Invitations
- ☐ Ring Bearer Pillow
- ☐ Programs
- ☐ Gifts (From Groom)
- ☐ Other Keepsakes

The Bridal Checklist

☐ Wedding Dress

☐ Veil & Hairpieces

☐ Shoes

☐ Necklace

☐ Earrings

☐ Other Jewelry

☐ Purse or Clutch

☐ Perfume

☐ Garter

☐ Wedding Rings

☐ Bouquets

☐ Invitations

☐ Ring Bearer Pillow

☐ Programs

☐ Gifts (From Groom)

☐ Other Keepsakes

The Bridal Checklist

- ☐ Wedding Dress
- ☐ Veil & Hairpieces
- ☐ Shoes
- ☐ Necklace
- ☐ Earrings
- ☐ Other Jewelry
- ☐ Purse or Clutch
- ☐ Perfume
- ☐ Garter
- ☐ Wedding Rings
- ☐ Bouquets
- ☐ Invitations
- ☐ Ring Bearer Pillow
- ☐ Programs
- ☐ Gifts (From Groom)
- ☐ Other Keepsakes

The Bridal Checklist

- ☐ Wedding Dress
- ☐ Veil & Hairpieces
- ☐ Shoes
- ☐ Necklace
- ☐ Earrings
- ☐ Other Jewelry
- ☐ Purse or Clutch
- ☐ Perfume
- ☐ Garter
- ☐ Wedding Rings

- ☐ Bouquets
- ☐ Invitations
- ☐ Ring Bearer Pillow
- ☐ Programs
- ☐ Gifts (From Groom)
- ☐ Other Keepsakes

The Bridal Checklist

- ☐ Wedding Dress
- ☐ Veil & Hairpieces
- ☐ Shoes
- ☐ Necklace
- ☐ Earrings
- ☐ Other Jewelry
- ☐ Purse or Clutch
- ☐ Perfume
- ☐ Garter
- ☐ Wedding Rings

- ☐ Bouquets
- ☐ Invitations
- ☐ Ring Bearer Pillow
- ☐ Programs
- ☐ Gifts (From Groom)
- ☐ Other Keepsakes

The Bridal Checklist

- ☐ Wedding Dress
- ☐ Veil & Hairpieces
- ☐ Shoes
- ☐ Necklace
- ☐ Earrings
- ☐ Other Jewelry
- ☐ Purse or Clutch
- ☐ Perfume
- ☐ Garter
- ☐ Wedding Rings

- ☐ Bouquets
- ☐ Invitations
- ☐ Ring Bearer Pillow
- ☐ Programs
- ☐ Gifts (From Groom)
- ☐ Other Keepsakes

The Bridal Checklist

- ☐ Wedding Dress
- ☐ Veil & Hairpieces
- ☐ Shoes
- ☐ Necklace
- ☐ Earrings
- ☐ Other Jewelry
- ☐ Purse or Clutch
- ☐ Perfume
- ☐ Garter
- ☐ Wedding Rings

- ☐ Bouquets
- ☐ Invitations
- ☐ Ring Bearer Pillow
- ☐ Programs
- ☐ Gifts (From Groom)
- ☐ Other Keepsakes

The Bridal Checklist

- ☐ Wedding Dress
- ☐ Veil & Hairpieces
- ☐ Shoes
- ☐ Necklace
- ☐ Earrings
- ☐ Other Jewelry
- ☐ Purse or Clutch
- ☐ Perfume
- ☐ Garter
- ☐ Wedding Rings

- ☐ Bouquets
- ☐ Invitations
- ☐ Ring Bearer Pillow
- ☐ Programs
- ☐ Gifts (From Groom)
- ☐ Other Keepsakes

The Bridal Checklist

- ☐ Wedding Dress
- ☐ Veil & Hairpieces
- ☐ Shoes
- ☐ Necklace
- ☐ Earrings
- ☐ Other Jewelry
- ☐ Purse or Clutch
- ☐ Perfume
- ☐ Garter
- ☐ Wedding Rings

- ☐ Bouquets
- ☐ Invitations
- ☐ Ring Bearer Pillow
- ☐ Programs
- ☐ Gifts (From Groom)
- ☐ Other Keepsakes

The Bridal Checklist

- ☐ Wedding Dress
- ☐ Veil & Hairpieces
- ☐ Shoes
- ☐ Necklace
- ☐ Earrings
- ☐ Other Jewelry
- ☐ Purse or Clutch
- ☐ Perfume
- ☐ Garter
- ☐ Wedding Rings

- ☐ Bouquets
- ☐ Invitations
- ☐ Ring Bearer Pillow
- ☐ Programs
- ☐ Gifts (From Groom)
- ☐ Other Keepsakes

The Bridal Checklist

☐ Wedding Dress	☐ Bouquets
☐ Veil & Hairpieces	☐ Invitations
☐ Shoes	☐ Ring Bearer Pillow
☐ Necklace	☐ Programs
☐ Earrings	☐ Gifts (From Groom)
☐ Other Jewelry	☐ Other Keepsakes
☐ Purse or Clutch	
☐ Perfume	
☐ Garter	
☐ Wedding Rings	

The Bridal Checklist

<table>
<tr><td>☐ Wedding Dress</td><td>☐ Bouquets</td></tr>
<tr><td>☐ Veil & Hairpieces</td><td>☐ Invitations</td></tr>
<tr><td>☐ Shoes</td><td>☐ Ring Bearer Pillow</td></tr>
<tr><td>☐ Necklace</td><td>☐ Programs</td></tr>
<tr><td>☐ Earrings</td><td>☐ Gifts (From Groom)</td></tr>
<tr><td>☐ Other Jewelry</td><td>☐ Other Keepsakes</td></tr>
<tr><td>☐ Purse or Clutch</td><td></td></tr>
<tr><td>☐ Perfume</td><td></td></tr>
<tr><td>☐ Garter</td><td></td></tr>
<tr><td>☐ Wedding Rings</td><td></td></tr>
</table>

The Bridal Checklist

☐ Wedding Dress	☐ Bouquets
☐ Veil & Hairpieces	☐ Invitations
☐ Shoes	☐ Ring Bearer Pillow
☐ Necklace	☐ Programs
☐ Earrings	☐ Gifts (From Groom)
☐ Other Jewelry	☐ Other Keepsakes
☐ Purse or Clutch	
☐ Perfume	
☐ Garter	
☐ Wedding Rings	

The Bridal Checklist

- ☐ Wedding Dress
- ☐ Veil & Hairpieces
- ☐ Shoes
- ☐ Necklace
- ☐ Earrings
- ☐ Other Jewelry
- ☐ Purse or Clutch
- ☐ Perfume
- ☐ Garter
- ☐ Wedding Rings

- ☐ Bouquets
- ☐ Invitations
- ☐ Ring Bearer Pillow
- ☐ Programs
- ☐ Gifts (From Groom)
- ☐ Other Keepsakes

The Bridal Checklist

- ☐ Wedding Dress
- ☐ Veil & Hairpieces
- ☐ Shoes
- ☐ Necklace
- ☐ Earrings
- ☐ Other Jewelry
- ☐ Purse or Clutch
- ☐ Perfume
- ☐ Garter
- ☐ Wedding Rings

- ☐ Bouquets
- ☐ Invitations
- ☐ Ring Bearer Pillow
- ☐ Programs
- ☐ Gifts (From Groom)
- ☐ Other Keepsakes

The Bridal Checklist

- ☐ Wedding Dress
- ☐ Veil & Hairpieces
- ☐ Shoes
- ☐ Necklace
- ☐ Earrings
- ☐ Other Jewelry
- ☐ Purse or Clutch
- ☐ Perfume
- ☐ Garter
- ☐ Wedding Rings

- ☐ Bouquets
- ☐ Invitations
- ☐ Ring Bearer Pillow
- ☐ Programs
- ☐ Gifts (From Groom)
- ☐ Other Keepsakes

The Bridal Checklist

- ☐ Wedding Dress
- ☐ Veil & Hairpieces
- ☐ Shoes
- ☐ Necklace
- ☐ Earrings
- ☐ Other Jewelry
- ☐ Purse or Clutch
- ☐ Perfume
- ☐ Garter
- ☐ Wedding Rings

- ☐ Bouquets
- ☐ Invitations
- ☐ Ring Bearer Pillow
- ☐ Programs
- ☐ Gifts (From Groom)
- ☐ Other Keepsakes

The Bridal Checklist

- [ ] Wedding Dress
- [ ] Veil & Hairpieces
- [ ] Shoes
- [ ] Necklace
- [ ] Earrings
- [ ] Other Jewelry
- [ ] Purse or Clutch
- [ ] Perfume
- [ ] Garter
- [ ] Wedding Rings

- [ ] Bouquets
- [ ] Invitations
- [ ] Ring Bearer Pillow
- [ ] Programs
- [ ] Gifts (From Groom)
- [ ] Other Keepsakes

The Bridal Checklist

<table>
<tr><td>☐ Wedding Dress</td><td>☐ Bouquets</td></tr>
<tr><td>☐ Veil & Hairpieces</td><td>☐ Invitations</td></tr>
<tr><td>☐ Shoes</td><td>☐ Ring Bearer Pillow</td></tr>
<tr><td>☐ Necklace</td><td>☐ Programs</td></tr>
<tr><td>☐ Earrings</td><td>☐ Gifts (From Groom)</td></tr>
<tr><td>☐ Other Jewelry</td><td>☐ Other Keepsakes</td></tr>
<tr><td>☐ Purse or Clutch</td><td></td></tr>
<tr><td>☐ Perfume</td><td></td></tr>
<tr><td>☐ Garter</td><td></td></tr>
<tr><td>☐ Wedding Rings</td><td></td></tr>
</table>

The Bridal Checklist

- ☐ Wedding Dress
- ☐ Veil & Hairpieces
- ☐ Shoes
- ☐ Necklace
- ☐ Earrings
- ☐ Other Jewelry
- ☐ Purse or Clutch
- ☐ Perfume
- ☐ Garter
- ☐ Wedding Rings

- ☐ Bouquets
- ☐ Invitations
- ☐ Ring Bearer Pillow
- ☐ Programs
- ☐ Gifts (From Groom)
- ☐ Other Keepsakes

The Bridal Checklist

- ☐ Wedding Dress
- ☐ Veil & Hairpieces
- ☐ Shoes
- ☐ Necklace
- ☐ Earrings
- ☐ Other Jewelry
- ☐ Purse or Clutch
- ☐ Perfume
- ☐ Garter
- ☐ Wedding Rings

- ☐ Bouquets
- ☐ Invitations
- ☐ Ring Bearer Pillow
- ☐ Programs
- ☐ Gifts (From Groom)
- ☐ Other Keepsakes

The Bridal Checklist

- [ ] Wedding Dress
- [ ] Veil & Hairpieces
- [ ] Shoes
- [ ] Necklace
- [ ] Earrings
- [ ] Other Jewelry
- [ ] Purse or Clutch
- [ ] Perfume
- [ ] Garter
- [ ] Wedding Rings
- [ ] Bouquets
- [ ] Invitations
- [ ] Ring Bearer Pillow
- [ ] Programs
- [ ] Gifts (From Groom)
- [ ] Other Keepsakes

The Bridal Checklist

- ☐ Wedding Dress
- ☐ Veil & Hairpieces
- ☐ Shoes
- ☐ Necklace
- ☐ Earrings
- ☐ Other Jewelry
- ☐ Purse or Clutch
- ☐ Perfume
- ☐ Garter
- ☐ Wedding Rings

- ☐ Bouquets
- ☐ Invitations
- ☐ Ring Bearer Pillow
- ☐ Programs
- ☐ Gifts (From Groom)
- ☐ Other Keepsakes

The Bridal Checklist

- ☐ Wedding Dress
- ☐ Veil & Hairpieces
- ☐ Shoes
- ☐ Necklace
- ☐ Earrings
- ☐ Other Jewelry
- ☐ Purse or Clutch
- ☐ Perfume
- ☐ Garter
- ☐ Wedding Rings

- ☐ Bouquets
- ☐ Invitations
- ☐ Ring Bearer Pillow
- ☐ Programs
- ☐ Gifts (From Groom)
- ☐ Other Keepsakes

The Bridal Checklist

- ☐ Wedding Dress
- ☐ Veil & Hairpieces
- ☐ Shoes
- ☐ Necklace
- ☐ Earrings
- ☐ Other Jewelry
- ☐ Purse or Clutch
- ☐ Perfume
- ☐ Garter
- ☐ Wedding Rings

- ☐ Bouquets
- ☐ Invitations
- ☐ Ring Bearer Pillow
- ☐ Programs
- ☐ Gifts (From Groom)
- ☐ Other Keepsakes

The Bridal Checklist

<table>
<tr><td>☐ Wedding Dress</td><td>☐ Bouquets</td></tr>
<tr><td>☐ Veil & Hairpieces</td><td>☐ Invitations</td></tr>
<tr><td>☐ Shoes</td><td>☐ Ring Bearer Pillow</td></tr>
<tr><td>☐ Necklace</td><td>☐ Programs</td></tr>
<tr><td>☐ Earrings</td><td>☐ Gifts (From Groom)</td></tr>
<tr><td>☐ Other Jewelry</td><td>☐ Other Keepsakes</td></tr>
<tr><td>☐ Purse or Clutch</td><td></td></tr>
<tr><td>☐ Perfume</td><td></td></tr>
<tr><td>☐ Garter</td><td></td></tr>
<tr><td>☐ Wedding Rings</td><td></td></tr>
</table>

The Bridal Checklist

- ☐ Wedding Dress
- ☐ Veil & Hairpieces
- ☐ Shoes
- ☐ Necklace
- ☐ Earrings
- ☐ Other Jewelry
- ☐ Purse or Clutch
- ☐ Perfume
- ☐ Garter
- ☐ Wedding Rings

- ☐ Bouquets
- ☐ Invitations
- ☐ Ring Bearer Pillow
- ☐ Programs
- ☐ Gifts (From Groom)
- ☐ Other Keepsakes

The Bridal Checklist

- ☐ Wedding Dress
- ☐ Veil & Hairpieces
- ☐ Shoes
- ☐ Necklace
- ☐ Earrings
- ☐ Other Jewelry
- ☐ Purse or Clutch
- ☐ Perfume
- ☐ Garter
- ☐ Wedding Rings

- ☐ Bouquets
- ☐ Invitations
- ☐ Ring Bearer Pillow
- ☐ Programs
- ☐ Gifts (From Groom)
- ☐ Other Keepsakes

The Bridal Checklist

- ☐ Wedding Dress
- ☐ Veil & Hairpieces
- ☐ Shoes
- ☐ Necklace
- ☐ Earrings
- ☐ Other Jewelry
- ☐ Purse or Clutch
- ☐ Perfume
- ☐ Garter
- ☐ Wedding Rings

- ☐ Bouquets
- ☐ Invitations
- ☐ Ring Bearer Pillow
- ☐ Programs
- ☐ Gifts (From Groom)
- ☐ Other Keepsakes

The Bridal Checklist

- ☐ Wedding Dress
- ☐ Veil & Hairpieces
- ☐ Shoes
- ☐ Necklace
- ☐ Earrings
- ☐ Other Jewelry
- ☐ Purse or Clutch
- ☐ Perfume
- ☐ Garter
- ☐ Wedding Rings
- ☐ Bouquets
- ☐ Invitations
- ☐ Ring Bearer Pillow
- ☐ Programs
- ☐ Gifts (From Groom)
- ☐ Other Keepsakes

The Bridal Checklist

- ☐ Wedding Dress
- ☐ Veil & Hairpieces
- ☐ Shoes
- ☐ Necklace
- ☐ Earrings
- ☐ Other Jewelry
- ☐ Purse or Clutch
- ☐ Perfume
- ☐ Garter
- ☐ Wedding Rings

- ☐ Bouquets
- ☐ Invitations
- ☐ Ring Bearer Pillow
- ☐ Programs
- ☐ Gifts (From Groom)
- ☐ Other Keepsakes

The Bridal Checklist

- ☐ Wedding Dress
- ☐ Veil & Hairpieces
- ☐ Shoes
- ☐ Necklace
- ☐ Earrings
- ☐ Other Jewelry
- ☐ Purse or Clutch
- ☐ Perfume
- ☐ Garter
- ☐ Wedding Rings

- ☐ Bouquets
- ☐ Invitations
- ☐ Ring Bearer Pillow
- ☐ Programs
- ☐ Gifts (From Groom)
- ☐ Other Keepsakes

The Bridal Checklist

- ☐ Wedding Dress
- ☐ Veil & Hairpieces
- ☐ Shoes
- ☐ Necklace
- ☐ Earrings
- ☐ Other Jewelry
- ☐ Purse or Clutch
- ☐ Perfume
- ☐ Garter
- ☐ Wedding Rings

- ☐ Bouquets
- ☐ Invitations
- ☐ Ring Bearer Pillow
- ☐ Programs
- ☐ Gifts (From Groom)
- ☐ Other Keepsakes

The Bridal Checklist

- ☐ Wedding Dress
- ☐ Veil & Hairpieces
- ☐ Shoes
- ☐ Necklace
- ☐ Earrings
- ☐ Other Jewelry
- ☐ Purse or Clutch
- ☐ Perfume
- ☐ Garter
- ☐ Wedding Rings

- ☐ Bouquets
- ☐ Invitations
- ☐ Ring Bearer Pillow
- ☐ Programs
- ☐ Gifts (From Groom)
- ☐ Other Keepsakes

The Bridal Checklist

- ☐ Wedding Dress
- ☐ Veil & Hairpieces
- ☐ Shoes
- ☐ Necklace
- ☐ Earrings
- ☐ Other Jewelry
- ☐ Purse or Clutch
- ☐ Perfume
- ☐ Garter
- ☐ Wedding Rings

- ☐ Bouquets
- ☐ Invitations
- ☐ Ring Bearer Pillow
- ☐ Programs
- ☐ Gifts (From Groom)
- ☐ Other Keepsakes

The Bridal Checklist

- [ ] Wedding Dress
- [ ] Veil & Hairpieces
- [ ] Shoes
- [ ] Necklace
- [ ] Earrings
- [ ] Other Jewelry
- [ ] Purse or Clutch
- [ ] Perfume
- [ ] Garter
- [ ] Wedding Rings

- [ ] Bouquets
- [ ] Invitations
- [ ] Ring Bearer Pillow
- [ ] Programs
- [ ] Gifts (From Groom)
- [ ] Other Keepsakes

www.ingramcontent.com/pod-product-compliance
Lightning Source LLC
Chambersburg PA
CBHW080723260726
48660CB00010B/3672